WHAT IF?

FIFTY DISCOVERIES
THAT CHANGED
THE WORLD

DIAN DINCIN BUCHMAN

and

SELI GROVES

SCHOLASTIC INC.
New York Toronto London Auckland Sydney

ISBN 0-590-41009-1

12 11 10 9 8 7 6 5 4 3 2   8 9/8 0 1 2 3/9

Printed in the U.S.A.   01

First Scholastic printing, December 1988

CONTENTS

Introduction

Just think what never would have happened if people never said, *What if? What if* I tried this? *What if* I looked at that in a different way?

There would never have been ice cream in a cone or photographs that don't fade or balloons that carry people gliding through the sky.

The stories in this book are about people who looked at things and wondered if they could make something else happen with what they saw. They took another look at an ordinary thing, and they asked, *"What if . . .?"* and went on to do something wonderful. They made an important association or connection. Their *What ifs* changed your life and mine for the better.

And if you haven't done so already, start taking a second look at the world around you, and ask, *What if?* It could be the most important question you ever asked.

Velcro:
THE VELVET HOOK

On a clear, warm, spring day in 1948, George de Mestral took a walk through a field area near his house in Switzerland.

When he returned home later that afternoon, his clothes were covered with thistle blossoms. He tried to brush them off, but it was impossible. He had to pick them off one by one, and as he did so, he wondered: "Why do they cling to the cloth as if they had invisible claws?"

Using a microscope, he examined several thistle blossoms carefully. He didn't find claws at the end of each petal, but he did find tiny hooks. He thought of how these little hooks had stuck to his clothes, and he wondered, "*What if* I could put tiny hooks on cloth strips so that they would cling together and act like fasteners?"

For eight years de Mestral worked on his idea before he was finally able to produce what he wanted. He named his invention Velcro, a combination of two French words: *velours*, meaning velvet, for the rough velvety feel of Velcro, and *crochet*, which means hook. This "velvet hook" is now used to fasten all kinds of things — even tennis shoes!

Rubber:

THE GOO THAT TURNED INTO SOMETHING GOOD!

Imagine turning your pencil upside down and trying to erase a mistake on a very hot day only to find you're rubbing your paper with goo! Or, on a very cold day, you find your eraser has cracked into little pieces.

Well, until a lucky accident in the workshop of Charles Goodyear in 1839, that was what always happened to rubber. It melted in the heat and cracked in the cold.

Since rubber was water repellent, the United States Post Office announced that if someone could find a process to make rubber useful in every temperature range, it would then be used in mail pouches to protect mail being sent across the country.

Charles Goodyear was one of thousands of inventors who worked to find that elusive process. He tried rubbing various chemicals into raw rubber to change its consistency. Nothing worked until one day when he added some sulfur to a batch of rubber. He got the same result: no change. He thought about adding another chemical later. As he reached up to put the batch on a shelf over a wood-burning stove, it slid out of the dish and fell onto the top of the hot stove. The sulfur in the rubber heated up. "What a terrible smell," he thought. "I'd better scrape the goo off before I do anything else."

To his surprise, there was no goo. The rubber didn't melt. It was soft, but firm. He thought, *"What if* it was the heat that made the difference?"

He tried rubbing other substances into the raw rubber and heating those combinations. But only the sulfur worked.

Goodyear named his process vulcanization, after Vulcan, the Roman god of volcanoes and fire.

Once rubber could be turned into a flexible and usable product with vulcanization, many things would be made of it, including one very special item invented by his son, Charles Goodyear, Jr. That was the world's first pair of sneakers.

Sneakers:

A BIG FEAT
FOR YOUR FEET

Charles Goodyear had discovered vulcanization in 1839. (See the story on page 4.) This was the process in which sulfur was mixed with raw rubber and heated. It made the rubber flexible and useful in all kinds of weather conditions.

One of the most popular products made with rubber after vulcanization was introduced were waterproof boots. These were especially useful for keeping people's feet dry not only in rain or

7

snow, but also when they had to slog through muddy fields.

But the boots were also heavy and hot. Goodyear's son, Charles, Jr., thought about a way to produce a lighter-weight waterproof boot with a rubber sole and a fabric top.

His friend, Elias Howe, had invented the sewing machine. (See page 80 for the story of the sewing machine.) He told young Goodyear that he had been able to develop a very strong needle that could sew soft leather strips to thick leather soles to make shoes.

Well, that's all Goodyear had to hear. Immediately, he thought to himself, "*What if* I used Elias' sewing machine to sew strips of canvas material to rubber soles to make lightweight, comfortable shoes that can keep people's feet dry?"

Charles Goodyear, Jr.'s idea worked. And that's how, in the 1870s, the first pair of sneakers was made.

Sandwich:

AN ENGLISH LORD IS IN YOUR LUNCHBOX!

John Montagu was a very busy man. He was an English nobleman in the 1700s, and one of his duties was to serve as head of the British Navy. When he relaxed, he played cards with his friends. And when he got into the middle of a game, he would stop for nothing — not even proper meals.

One evening his servant brought a tray of sliced meats and bread. Lord Montagu and his friends were playing a game that required them to put some cards on the table and cover those cards with other cards.

Montagu said, *"What if* I did the same thing with this food?" His friends smiled. What did he mean by that? "I'll show you," he said. He picked up one slice of bread and covered it with a thick slice of meat and then put another slice of bread on top of that. "There," he said. "Now I have a perfect meal to enjoy while playing cards. And, notice," he added, "that I can hold my cards in one hand and my meal in the other."

Montagu's idea caught on quickly. His admiring friends named his quick meal invention after him.

All right. So you say you never ate a "montagu," and you certainly never had a lord montagu in your lunchbox? Well, his friends thought his invention was so special, they used the special part of his full name which was John Montagu, the Earl of Sandwich.

Hot Air Balloons:
FULL OF HOT AIR

Brothers Jacques and Joseph Mont-golfier lived in France in the 1700s. They loved to fly kites. When the wind was high, they would let out their kite strings and watch their "paper birds" soar up into the skies. When the wind began to die down, they would skillfully guide the falling kites through the air so that they wouldn't catch in the tree branches.

One day, the wind died so suddenly, there was no time to guide the kite down. They watched in horror as it fell straight toward a fire in which a farmer was burning old straw. But just as the kite was about to tumble into the flames, it stopped falling and floated in the heated air over the fire. The boys stared in astonishment, then shouted with glee. Their kite was safe!

When they grew up they turned from flying kites to building big balloons. They planned to put baskets or gondolas beneath the balloons large enough to carry them high over the countryside. But they had a big problem to solve: How could they get the balloons to rise in a low wind, and stay up if the wind died?

After many tries and many failures, the brothers remembered the kite that floated above the fire. They thought, "What if we could build a carefully tended fire in a gondola beneath one of our big balloons? That would heat the air which would rise up to fill the balloon. Then, the balloon would stay up as long as we kept the fire going."

They got into the gondola of one of their big balloons and made a small fire in a metal pot set beneath the opening of the balloon. As the fire heated the air, the balloon rose, and Jacques and Joseph Montgolfier, who had loved to fly kites, became the first people to fly under their own power.

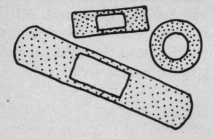

BAND-AIDS:
SHE WAS A REAL CUT-UP

Did you ever meet people who just can't seem to keep from hurting themselves no matter what? They trip over their own feet or they drop things on their toes. They're often called accident-prone.

Josephine Dickinson was one of those accident-prone people. Good thing her husband, Joseph, worked for Johnson & Johnson, a big company that made gauze bandages and adhesive tape. He could buy these materials at a discount so his wife always had plenty on hand to use when she cut herself or banged her knee or scraped her elbow.

She had so many accidents that her husband started cutting different lengths of bandage and small snippets of adhesive tape to keep the bandages on her next cuts or bruises.

As he snipped, he thought, *"What if I cut the bandage into different lengths and put them down in the middle of longer pieces of adhesive tape? Then I could cover any cut or bruise my wife might have in just a few seconds."*

The next day Josephine cut her finger while slicing carrots. She reached for one of her husband's "quick" bandages and very quickly covered her wound.

Dickinson took his idea to work, and in 1924, Johnson & Johnson introduced the world's most famous bandage: the BAND-AID.

Telescope and Microscope:

WHAT BIG EYES
WE HAVE

Can you imagine living in a world where you were taught that nothing exists if you can't see it? That would mean never knowing about things too small — or too far away — to see with your naked eyes.

The eyes of the world were opened, however, with the invention of two remarkable devices: the telescope and the microscope. Here are the stories of how these two marvelous inventions came into our lives.

1. THE TELESCOPE

In the late 1500s and early 1600s, the use of eyeglasses, or spectacles as they were called in those days, was growing. Glass lens grinding had become a highly skilled profession, and Holland, which had the most skilled lens grinders in the world, soon became the center of the spectacle trade.

One story about the origin of the telescope centers around one such Dutch lens grinder and spectacle maker named Hans Lippershey, who lived in the town of Middleburg around 1600. He was working with two thick glass lenses — one convex, one concave — that he intended to grind down for two pairs of spectacles when two children came into his workshop. One of them picked up the two different lenses and placed one on top of the other. The boy held them up to his eye and looked out through the window. What he saw startled him so much that he almost dropped both lenses!

"The weather vane on top of the church steeple jumped up and came right at me!" he told his friend.

17

The other boy shook his head. "That is not possible. The weather vane didn't move."

"Look for yourself." The first boy gave his friend the two lenses.

This time, the second boy almost dropped the lenses. He, too, thought he saw the weather vane come so close, he felt he could reach out and touch it.

The boys rushed to tell Hans Lippershey what they had seen. Lippershey looked through the lenses, and sure enough, he saw what the boys saw. But because he knew how glass can magnify objects, he understood what had happened.

It wasn't the church steeple or the weather vane that moved: When the thick lenses were put together, they acted like a powerful magnifier.

Lippershey scanned his workshop and saw a hollow tube resting on a nearby table.

He thought, *"What if* I placed the lenses, one on top of the other, in the tube so that they could stay together without slipping?"

He did this, and was delighted at how

easy it was now to focus on whatever he wanted to look at.

He marveled at how close Mr. van Brinker's bakery seemed to be — yet it was over two blocks away. The canal, which was even further away, seemed so close when he looked at it that he took a step back, as if he thought he might fall into it.

Hans devoted the next eight years to improving his invention.

Meanwhile, over in Venice, Italy, Galileo Galilei, the instrument maker and professor of mathematics, was studying the new science of motion. He would spend hours staring up at the heavens watching how the planets moved. He heard about Lippershey's device for magnifying faraway objects.

Once he knew about the concept, his brilliantly inventive mind worked out a way to improve it so that it could be used to "see" even farther than Lippershey's most advanced version.

In 1609 Galileo called his new device a telescope, which means "far watcher" from two Greek words — *tele*, meaning far, and *scope*, meaning to watch.

2. THE MICROSCOPE

People with a strong sense of scientific curiosity are always looking for new ways to do things, and new ways to use things. So, we shouldn't be surprised to learn that when Galileo wasn't using his new telescope to see things far away, he would think, *"What if* I turned this telescope onto something near instead of far?"

He focused it on a fly that was walking on the underside of a pane of glass. What he saw shocked him so much, he later recorded that he thought he was looking at a hairy monster with hooks on its feet. He realized he had seen the insect the way no human being had seen it before.

The telescope, of course, is not a microscope, although both instruments are similarly made. But Galileo was the first person we know of to use the telescope as a microscope.

No one knows for sure who invented the first microscope — a word that comes from two Greek words — *micro*, meaning small, and *scope*, meaning to watch. Some people think it was a Dutch spectacle maker named Jansen who first took credit for it. But no one really did very much with it until a Dutch draper — a dealer in cloth — named Antonie van Leeuwenhoek did something remarkable in 1674.

Dutch drapers used magnifying glasses to examine fabric for imperfections not easily seen by the naked eye. Leeuwenhoek devised a more efficient way to use the glass by putting it between two metal plates through which he pulled lengths of cloth. This simple device was the first of 247 microscope models which Leeuwenhoek would build in his lifetime.

He started improving his draper's device with stronger and stronger lenses. One September day in 1674, while walking along the shores of a marshy lake, he suddenly thought, *"What if* I used my glass scope to look into a drop of water?"

He brought home a sample of the lake water. After focusing his scope on a drop of that water, he looked through the glass and was astonished at what he saw. "There are tiny eels swimming about in the water," he wrote.

He called the creatures *animalcules*. He didn't know it then, but he had just become the first human being to peer into the invisible world of bacteria. This moment of discovery also marked humanity's first step toward finding the cause — and thus the cure — of many of the world's most feared diseases.

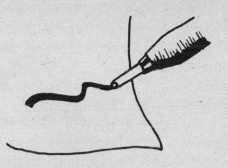

Ballpoint Pen:
WRITING WITH A BALL

People used to write with pens which had to be dipped over and over in ink or with fountain pens that they filled up with ink.

Sometimes the ink would spill — and sometimes the fountain pens would leak.

One day in Hungary, in 1938, a newspaperman named Biro visited a print shop. He noticed that when the papers came out of the press, the ink the printer used was dry, not wet or smudgy.

He thought to himself, "That would be a great ink to have inside a pen!

What if I could make a pen that could carry a quick drying ink inside of it — the way a fountain pen carries regular ink inside of *it*?"

He worked out the first model, but the ink didn't come through the point. He had to make a completely different point. Instead of a long, thin one, he used a round ball that *spread* the ink over the paper like a paint roller spreads paint over a wall.

In 1940 when the Nazis invaded Hungary, Biro escaped to Argentina, where in 1943 he patented his ingenious pen. Meanwhile, the English government had a problem with the pens used by the pilots of the Royal Air Force. The high altitudes at which the planes flew often caused these pens to leak. The pilots began using Biro's new pen with its quick drying ink and its ballpoint. No leaks! Soon the ballpoint Biro pen was used all over the world.

Condenser:

JAMES WATT AND THE TEA KETTLE THAT FLIPPED ITS LID

Young Jamie Watt was just six years old that day in 1742 when he sat in his mother's kitchen in Scotland and watched her tea kettle as the water inside boiled away.

As the water boiled, it created steam. As the steam rose, it forced the kettle lid to rise as well. As some of the steam escaped, the kettle lid fell back.

When the steam rose once more, the lid rose as well. As long as the water boiled and made steam, the lid went up and down and up and down.

When James Watt grew up he worked with all types of steam machines and gained fame as one of the world's finest engineers.

In 1765 he was asked to check out an engine that wasn't working as well as its designer intended.

Watt took the engine apart and soon saw what the problem was: Too much steam was escaping from the steam cylinder before it could make the engine work more efficiently.

He thought back to the way the lid on his mother's tea kettle moved up and down as the steam rose.

"What if," he thought, "I could put a lid on the cylinder to control the steam flow?"

Watt's idea led to his inventing the first condenser which led to his next invention, the first really efficient steam piston.

Today, some pistons drive trains; some help propel airplanes; some drive cars and boats, and some generate electricity. And all of this is possible because James Watt recalled how his mother's tea kettle flipped its lid.

Watt also worked out systems for measuring electricity. We use his name for some of those measurements. For example, how bright is the bulb in your lamp? Is it forty watts? Seventy-five watts? Or what watts?

Ice Cream Sundaes:

MAKING THE ICE CREAM LAST

Do you like sprinkles or nuts or hot fudge or butterscotch or whipped cream and a cherry on the top of your sundae? Or would you prefer all of these toppings on your pistachio-strawberry-vanilla ice cream?

Well, we wouldn't be enjoying these treats today if a certain Mr. Smithson of Wisconsin hadn't run low on his ice cream supply one Sunday in 1890.

But while he was low on ice cream, he had plenty of fruit, heavy cream just right for whipping, and chocolate syrup on hand for making chocolate milk.

What he had to do was make his low supply of ice cream last. He thought, *"What if* I gave my customers smaller helpings of ice cream, and to make up for the smaller amounts, I'll top each serving with fruit salad and syrup and dollops of whipped cream."

His customers loved Smithson's new ice cream creation. Soon people began asking for the "Sunday ice cream" on other days of the week.

Smithson, however, had to change the name of his dish from Sunday to sundae because some very religious people complained that they didn't like using the name of the Lord's day that way.

SCUBA:

THE MAN WITH
THREE LUNGS

In 1943 Frenchman Jacques Yves Cousteau, who loved to dive, found a way to dive deeper, and stay down longer, without wearing a clunky diving suit and a helmet that looked like a space alien's head.

Cousteau had been searching for years to find a way he could go down into the sea and swim as freely as a fish. He knew that if he could do that, many of the ocean's secrets would start opening up for him.

One day he saw a seal break through the water near his home. She put her head up and took a huge gulp of air before diving again. Cousteau thought about the fact that the seal, like us, is a mammal. Yet she can swim beneath the water for far longer than any person. He wondered why.

A marine biologist told Cousteau that a seal's lungs can expand to hold extra air.

Cousteau thought, "Just like a third lung! Of course! *What if* I, too, had a third lung? Could I then stay underwater for a long time, too?"

He designed a "third lung," which he called an AQUALUNG. It was an air-filled metal tank he strapped to his back. His air supply came through a hose connected from his mouth to the tank.

He dived into the water and gasped in wonder as he descended into a world filled with beauty and magic. "This is incredible," he said to himself. "I will spend my life learning the secrets of the deep."

Thanks to the AQUALUNG, also

known as the SCUBA (which stands for *S*elf-*C*ontained *U*nderwater *B*reathing *A*pparatus), millions of trained divers have shared Cousteau's wonder-filled exploration of the sea.

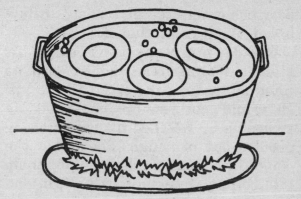

Bagel:

THE BAKER WHO USED
HIS NOODLE

Many years ago, the story goes, a greedy king in a small European country decided to raise taxes. But he had already taxed almost everything in the kingdom, except for the ovens that belonged to the Jewish bakers. Realizing this he called in every Jewish baker and said from that moment on they would have to pay a tax each time they used their ovens. The bakers were shocked. They couldn't afford to pay the tax! And if they raised prices their poor customers couldn't afford to buy bread. What could they do?

One day one of the bakers sat in his kitchen feeling very sad because he could no longer bake bread and sell it. He would soon lose his bake shop. He sighed as he watched his wife making noodles out of dough. She rolled the dough into small circles and put them into boiling water to cook up firm and tasty.

The baker thought, "My wife is using dough for noodles. I use another kind of dough for my bread. My wife rolls her noodle dough and boils it. Well, *what if* I rolled some of my dough into rings and boiled it, too?"

He tried it. His little dough rings bounced merrily in the boiling water. When they had plumped up into firm doughnut shapes, he knew they were done. He took them out and tasted the world's first bagel. It was chewy and delicious!

The new treat got its name, bagel, from a related word, *beignet*, which in French means something rounded or bowed and is the French word for doughnut.

Word spread about the boiled bread rings. The king was so impressed, he cancelled the tax. Today bagels are made the same way, but after they're boiled, they're put into an oven to brown.

Braille:

THE TEENAGER WHO TAUGHT THE BLIND TO READ

Louis Braille was only three years old when, in 1812, a tragic accident in his father's shop in France blinded him for life.

When he was ten years old, Louis' father suggested that since Louis had shown a definite talent for music, he should learn how to play several instruments so that he could make a living as a musician.

Young Louis agreed that that was a good idea. But he also wanted to learn to read and write.

Mr. Braille took Louis to the National Institute for Blind Children in Paris. There blind students could read by passing their fingers over large raised letters in any one of the Institute's fourteen books that weighed over twenty pounds each.

Louis found it difficult to handle the books, and the writing system was almost impossible to read. He wondered, could he find a better system?

When Louis was fifteen, Charles Barbier, a captain in the French army, came to see him. Barbier brought Louis his new invention, called night writing. It was a system of twelve dots and dashes that could be set down in raised type on very thin paper, and could be read with fingers in total darkness. Darkness was very important for Barbier's artillery soldiers. If they lit a match to read their orders, their position would be given away to the enemy.

Captain Barbier wanted someone to help him refine his system so that it would be easier to both write and read. He felt Louis would be the right person for the job.

Braille set to work on Barbier's invention and immediately thought, "*What if* this could be adapted for use by blind people?"

A year later, when he was just sixteen, Braille had worked out a simplified dots system using six raised points in different combinations.

In 1829 he published the first book of thirty-two in what would be called "The Braille System." A whole new world of reading was now open for the blind. They could study mathematics and other subjects that everyone else read in books that were smaller and easier to handle than the great big volumes that Braille first found when he arrived at the Institute.

Braille went on to devise Braille symbols for music as well. Before his system was put into use, blind musicians learned their music by ear. Now, they could sit in with orchestras, and by using their fingertips, read the score along with the other members of the group.

Windshield Wipers:

A TRANSPORTATION BREAKTHROUGH

Mary Anderson gritted her teeth as the New York City trolley car screeched to a halt. This was the fourth time the driver had to go out into the heavy rain to wipe away the water running down the window. "At this rate," she said to herself, "it will take an hour just to go ten blocks."

It was just as bad in winter when the driver had to get out every few blocks to scrape away the ice and snow on the window.

"There's got to be a way to clean the windows from inside," Anderson thought. Then she remembered how she had washed her own windows back home in Alabama. She had tied a sponge on the end of a stick, guiding the stick as the sponge washed the glass panes clean.

She thought, *"What if* I made something like that for the trolley car drivers?"

Anderson tried different materials. Finally, she tied a long length of hard rubber onto a pole that worked perfectly. It swept away rainwater and could also scrape away snow and ice.

She worked out a way to attach her "window wiper" to the outside of the trolley with a lever that the driver could operate from inside.

Mary Anderson's window wiper was installed in a trolley car in 1902. It was a success and was later adapted for use on cars, buses, trains, and planes.

Zipper:

HOW THE ZIPPER
ZAPPED THE BUTTON
HOOK

Whitcomb Judson was an inventor. His friends used to say that all you had to say to Judson was, I wish there was a way to do this or that, and soon Judson had invented a machine that did this or that — and did it very well.

Judson had a friend with a bad back. Each time his friend had to bend over to fasten his shoes with a button hook, which was the way shoes were fastened one hundred years ago, it was very painful for him.

Judson thought, "I wonder if I could invent a fastener that my friend could use without hurting his back."

He looked around his workshop to find something he could adapt into a new invention. He spotted a bicycle gear he had repaired that morning and recalled how the teeth on the gears fit together. This was called "meshing." This was the inspiration he needed. He thought, *What if* I made a special sort of gear system for fastening shoes?"

He came up with the idea of a facing row of hooks and eyes which could be pulled together with a slide handle. He took out a patent on his new slide fastener in 1893.

Later a man named Gideon Sundback decided to mesh interlocking metal teeth instead of the hooks and eyes. The invention was used on all sorts of things including rubber boots and clothing. People were so impressed by the fact that they only needed to use one hand to fasten things so quickly, in a zip, they said, that they nicknamed it the zipper.

Stethoscope:
DOCTOR, WHAT BIG EARS YOU HAVE!

A stethoscope makes it possible for your doctor's ears to hear more than they would otherwise.

When a doctor puts a stethoscope on your back or chest, she or he is listening to noises inside your body that reveal a lot about you, including how strong your heartbeat is. There are also certain other sounds the doctor hears that convey important information about your health.

The stethoscope was invented in Paris

in the early 1800s by a doctor named Dr. Rene Laënnec, while he was sitting with a young patient. He tried many times to listen to her heartbeat, but it was so faint, that no matter how many times he put his ear to her chest, he hardly heard anything at all.

But he did hear the voices of several children who were playing outside the window. They were shouting at each other through an old hollow tree trunk. Dr. Laënnec recalled that when he was a child, he and his friends played the same game, and when they shouted into the hollow tree, their voices came out loud and strong at each end. He thought, *"What if* I made a hollow tube and held it to my little patient's chest? Would I hear her heartbeat more loudly and clearly?"

Dr. Laënnec picked up a sheet of paper and rolled it into a tube. He put one end against his ear and the other on the little girl's chest. It worked! He could hear the sound of her heart beating clearly.

Later Dr. Laënnec, who played the flute, plugged the holes in one of his instruments and made the first wooden stethoscope. This first "magic flute" was so successful in helping Dr. Laënnec diagnose illness in patients, other doctors soon began using stethoscopes as well.

Coffee:

THE WORLD'S FIRST CUP
OF COFFEE

In the year 850 in a small Ethiopian village called Kava, a goatherd named Kaldi often took his goats to a place in the mountains where a certain type of bush with bright red berries grew.

Kaldi noticed that every time his goats ate those berries, they became frisky and he found it hard to get them to settle down.

One cold night, the story goes, Kaldi found himself nodding off although he knew he had to stay awake to protect the many newborn kids in the herd from prowling animals. He thought, "*What if* I ate some of those berries that made the goats so frisky?"

He picked a handful from the bush and tried to bite into them but they were too hard. So he boiled them to soften them. When the berries were soft, he ate them and then drank the water in which they were boiled. Before he knew it, he felt as wide awake as if he had just slept the night through.

He took some berries home with him and told everyone how they helped keep him awake during the long cold night.

The villagers named the berries and the drink they made from it after their village, Kava. In time the name changed according to the way people in different countries pronounced it. In France and Spain it was called café; in Germany, kaffee; in Russia, kofe, and in English, coffee.

Shatter-Resistant Glass:

THE GLASS SANDWICH

"Butterfingers! That's what I am," said Edouard Benedictus to himself as he felt the flask of liquid celluloid slip out of his hands. He closed his eyes. "What a mess it will be: glass pieces everywhere. How could I have been so clumsy?"

But when the French scientist opened his eyes that day in 1903, there were no pieces of glass around his laboratory. The flask had broken, but the liquid celluloid inside acted like glue keeping each piece of glass stuck to the edges of every other piece of glass. It looked like a glass jigsaw puzzle that had been glued together.

He thought, "If the glass hadn't scattered because just one side had been coated with the celluloid, *what if* I coated *both* sides of a glass sheet with celluloid? Would the glass sheet stay in one piece?"

He tried many ways to coat both sides, but none worked. One day, the story is, while having a sandwich for lunch he got an idea. "*What if* I made a glass sandwich by putting liquid celluloid between two pieces of glass?"

It worked! His new glass was shatter-resistant — it was almost unbreakable — and was soon used to make shatterproof glass doors, skyscraper windows, windshields, and eventually, bulletproof glass and eyeglasses.

Silk:

THE SECRET OF CATERPILLAR "THREAD"

Five thousand years ago, Si Ling-chi, the Empress of China, sat in her garden under her favorite mulberry tree while her ladies-in-waiting began preparing her afternoon tea.

She looked at the cocoons clinging to several tree branches and thought of how the caterpillars inside would one day emerge as fluttering moths.

As the water boiled in a big open pot, a strong wind came up. Some of the cocoons were blown into the pot. The Empress' ladies were upset. But before they could pour the water out and start a new pot boiling, the Empress stopped them. "Look," she said, pointing to the cocoons.

The ladies stared. Each cocoon had begun to unravel. Soon the pot was filled with masses of shining strands hundreds of feet long.

Si Ling-chi ordered one of her ladies to pick up some of the strands and give them to her. She could hardly believe how thin, yet how strong each thread was. Try as she might, she couldn't pull any one of them apart with her bare hands.

Si Ling-chi had an idea, "*What if* we could weave these strong, shining strands into cloth?"

She called in her weavers and ordered them to go to work. When they returned, they carried a length of shining fabric and gave it to the Empress. She called it "the cloth of the gods." We know it as silk.

The Empress ordered that the three secrets for making silk must never leave China:

First, no one could reveal that it was the mulberry tree caterpillar, or "worm," that spun the cocoon from which the silk threads would be unraveled.

Second, no one could reveal that it was only by putting the cocoons into boiling water that the threads would unravel without breaking.

Third, no one could reveal that the only thing the mulberry tree caterpillar would eat were mulberry leaves.

Si Ling-chi's secret stayed safe for three thousand years before other countries finally learned how to raise silk worms and make silk from their cocoons.

Tea Bags:
A TEA PARTY IN A BAG

If the Mad Hatter had had tea bags, the tea party Alice went to in Wonderland might have been very different. The tea would have been made quickly and with no fuss and everyone would have had more time to talk and have fun. But in those days, there were no tea bags. And if it hadn't been for a tea merchant named Thomas Sullivan who lived in New York in the early 1900s, perhaps we wouldn't have tea bags today.

Thomas Sullivan wanted to send his tea samples around the country in hopes of getting new orders for them. The way all tea merchants did this was to wrap a teaspoon of loose tea in some paper, seal it, and send it off in a package. But often, when the packages were opened, the loose tea would spill out, and since no one could sample it, the merchant would lose an order.

One day, the story goes, Sullivan watched a woman washing a silk shirt. The water just seemed to flow through the silk. He thought, *"What if* I sent out tea samples in small silk bags and told the store owners to put each bag in a cup and pour boiling water over it and let it brew?"

His idea worked. Not only did he get orders from people everywhere to send boxes of his teas to them, he also got requests for more tea in silk bags, so the store owners could sell tea in the new bags to their customers, who loved the ease of making tea this way.

Safety Pin:
KEEPING CLOTHES CLOSED!

Walter Hunt, an inventor, owed a friend some money. Knowing that Walter could invent anything he wanted to, the friend said, "To pay me back, make me an invention."

"All right," Hunt answered.

After his friend left, Hunt was bending and unbending a long brass wire when he thought, "Ummm, what can I do with this wire?"

Then he remembered how much he admired the art of ancient Greece, and how intrigued he was by a brass fastener the Greeks used three thousand years ago to fasten their clothes so that they draped in beautiful, even folds. The pin had been made of a brass wire that was hooked on one end.

"Ummmm," Hunt thought. "I wonder if I can make a pin with this wire that can fasten clothes quickly, easily, and safely."

He made a fastener out of the wire by hooking one end and bending the other over so that it fit into the hook.

Then he saw someone wearing a hood passing outside of his window. He thought, "*What if* I bent the hook end again so that it forms a small hood? Then when the pointy end fits in, the hood would cover it, and the point wouldn't stick anyone."

That's exactly what he did, and that's exactly how the world's first safety pin was invented in 1849.

Hunt never collected on his patent — he gave it, instead, to his friend.

Saving the Earth:
NO SILENT SPRING

No more birds? Ever? Gone for good? It can't happen. Can it?

Well, perhaps if Rachel Carson hadn't wondered why each spring there were fewer songbirds coming to nest in her backyard, we would be facing a world without birds, without any clean water, or beautiful wildlife at all.

Dr. Rachel Carson was a biologist, a scientist who studies life. During the 1950s she became concerned about the disappearance of the birds. She learned that many birds were laying eggs with such thin shells, the eggs broke before the baby birds could hatch. She began studying why this was happening and soon found that fish and other wildlife were also disappearing.

Dr. Carson's reports showed a very curious fact: The disappearance began the year after farmers around the world started using a powerful insect killer on their crops called DDT. She thought, "Birds eat insects and grain. *What if* it is the DDT that is killing the birds that ate the insects or the grain from those sprayed fields? And, *what if* it is DDT that makes the birds' eggshells so thin? And, *what if* DDT spray is poisoning the streams and killing the animals that drink that water, and the fish that live in it?"

People scoffed. DDT, they said, killed harmful insects. But Dr. Carson found proof that DDT also killed helpful insects and other forms of life. Her book, *Silent Spring* alerted the world to DDT's dangers and led to DDT being banned. Her efforts also started a whole new environmental movement which continues the fight to save the earth today.

Daguerreotype:
THE KEY THAT OPENED UP YOUR VERY OWN TIME MACHINE

If you own a camera, you own a time machine.

A camera makes a record of something that happens at a certain time by taking a photograph of the event. Each time you look at the picture, you go back to when it was taken, and you can relive the very moment the photo was snapped.

But it took a long time for photographs to be made that lasted beyond a few weeks or maybe years. Up until the mid-1830s, every time a photo was made, it would soon fade. In those days they didn't use film. The picture was exposed, instead, on different types of metal plates. And different types of chemicals would be put on the plates to produce pictures. But nothing really worked to make the picture last. They all soon faded.

One day in 1839 a young French photographer named Louis Jacques Mande Daguerre left a desk key on an uncoated plate which he kept in a cabinet. The cabinet also held chemicals. The next day he picked up the key from the uncoated plate and found the key's image on it. How could this be? He looked around. Nothing had spilled. But the stopper on a bottle of mercury was loose. He thought, "*What if* the mercury fumes that leaked out had coated the plate? Would that cause this to happen?"

He used the mercury fumes several more times, and to his delight he found he could make photographs that didn't fade. That key certainly opened up a time machine. Because his photographs didn't fade, we can take pictures today that people may see 150 years from now, just as we can look at Daguerre's photos, called Daguerreotypes (də'gerō-tīps), taken 150 years ago.

Cereal:
THE FIRST INSTANT BREAKFASTS

The perkiest man in Denver, Colorado in the 1890s was Mr. Henry D. Perky, who said he got his energy from having a good breakfast cereal every morning. But in those days, it could take almost an hour to prepare cereal. You had to stand and stir and stand and stir as it cooked. Most people just didn't have time for cereal in the morning.

One day Perky met a man who had stomach problems. This man would boil wheat grains and then soak the boiled wheat in milk. Perky thought, *"What if* I took those wheat grains, and instead of boiling them to make them easy to eat, I put them through a shredder to make them easier to eat without cooking?"

Perky's idea led to the first shredded wheat cereal. He found people everywhere eager to buy this new healthy breakfast product that didn't take forever to prepare.

A doctor named William Kellogg in Battle Creek, Michigan heard about Perky's shredded wheat. He thought, *"What if* I took wheat and corn and flattened them to make flakes?" His idea also worked, and soon people were buying his cereal, too. Before long almost every home in America had a box of Dr. Kellogg's Corn Flakes on the breakfast table.

Jane Goodall:
JANE SEE, JANE DO

Jane Goodall, a young English zoologist, went to Africa in 1960 to study chimpanzees in their natural surroundings. She hoped to be allowed to enter one of their groups so she could see, firsthand, how they really lived.

Chimpanzees had always made it very clear that they weren't issuing any invitations for any human beings to join one of their groups. When a researcher would try, the chimps would either flee or grimace menacingly, indicating they were prepared to fight to keep the intruders out.

When Goodall arrived in Tanzania, she made her way to an area where she was told a group, also called a "population," of chimpanzees was living. She set up an observation post where the chimps could see her, yet far enough away so they would not feel threatened by her.

For a year she watched them from that location until she felt they had grown accustomed to her and might let her move closer to them. But whenever she tried to cut the distance between them, they would move away.

She held bananas out to them, but they still kept their distance. Sometimes, though, a little chimp's curiosity would get the better of him, and he would start to move toward her. But the baby's mother or older sister would pull the youngster back.

Goodall realized her problem: She was an outsider who couldn't buy her way in just with bananas. She began to wonder if they would ever let any human being into their group. She thought, "I suppose they just don't *trust* people." Then she realized she had just said the magic word: *trust*. She thought, "*What if* I got them to trust me by trying to look and move and act more like them?"

She experimented by walking more like a chimp, with her knees bent and her arms dangling. She realized that when she was standing, she was much taller than the chimps. So she sat more often, making it easier for the smaller animals to look right at her in a real eyeball-to-eyeball encounter.

She also ate her bananas chimp-style — stuffing as much of the fruit into her mouth as she could at one bite. She left bunches of bananas around and soon a few bolder chimps came closer and touched her and let her touch them back. A bond of trust was being established as Goodall and the chimps got to know each other. Before long they let her enter their group and become part of their daily lives.

Jane Goodall spent twenty years studying chimpanzees. What she learned about them also taught us a lot about ourselves: After all, they are our closest animal kingdom cousins.

Ice Cream Cones:
A NEW SCOOP

In 1904 the city of St. Louis, Missouri put on one of the biggest fairs ever held anywhere.

Charles Menches was one of the many people who were there to sell refreshments to the fairgoers. He sold ice cream, and the hotter it got, the more dishes of ice cream he sold. At the end of a busy day, he always had fewer dishes left than he started with. Some broke when they were being washed. Some dropped to the floor and were cracked. And some just disappeared. But Menches never worried about that: His supplier always turned up with a new supply every day.

On one especially hot July day, Menches opened his stand prepared to face a very busy day. He needed lots of new dishes, but the supplier was late. Menches was down to a very low number of plates before noon. What, he wondered, would he do when the demand for ice cream increased with the arrival of the large noontime crowd?

His friend in the stand next to his, a man named Ernest Hamwi from Syria, was selling Zalabia, a sort of flat, crisp wafer that was popular in the Middle East. Menches thought he'd buy one of them for his lunch while he tried to think of a way to handle his disappearing dish problem. As he held the Zalabia, he noticed how easily it folded. It reminded him of how colored sheets of paper were rolled into cones to hold candies as birthday party favors when he was a little boy.

He thought, "*What if* I rolled the Zalabia into cones and put the ice cream into them?"

The idea was a fabulous success. People not only could eat the "dish" in which the ice cream was served, they could also walk around and enjoy the fair while enjoying their ice cream treat.

The Telephone:

THERE'S A VERY BIG EAR IN YOUR HOUSE!

Because Alexander Graham Bell was one of the few people in the world in the 1870s who knew how ears picked up and carried sound, he also knew how to make the first telephone.

Bell knew acoustics, the science of sound. That's why he could teach deaf people who never heard their own voices to speak. He also invented things and worked with an assistant named Thomas Watson.

One of Bell's inventions accidentally led to the telephone. What he planned to do was make a new kind of telegraph to send musical notes instead of just dots and dashes over the wires. It was a sort of electric harmonica which he called a "harmonic telegraph" in which an electric current would make the reeds inside vibrate. The vibration would send musical tones over a wire.

One day when Bell and Watson were testing the telegraph, Bell sat in one room with a receiver. Watson was in another room ready to send the music. But instead of music, Bell heard a jangling noise. Watson shouted out from the door, "It's broken. I'll have to take it apart."

But a "bell" went off in Bell's head. He rushed into the other room. "Don't do that," Bell said. "I think I know what happened."

While Watson only heard noise, Bell had a good idea about what caused the noise. He peered into the telegraph. "That's it," he said. His hunch was right! One of the reeds was stuck. When it vibrated, it set off all the other reeds causing the jangle. Bell muttered to himself, "Just like an eardrum." Because he knew what eardrums do in our ears, he had a good idea of how to use a reed in the same way. So, when Bell made that connection in his mind, he thought, *"What if* I built a device with a diaphragm made of a thin piece of iron that would vibrate like an eardrum? I wonder if it would carry the human voice through wires from one place to another?" Bell's excitement rose. He knew he was on the right track. One day in 1876 he finished the device. It was time to test it. He sat in his laboratory and asked Watson to sit in another room and wait by an open receiver. Then, the magical moment arrived: Watson heard Bell's voice coming out of the receiver. "Watson," he said, "come here, I need you."

Thomas Watson had just received the first telephone call!

The Cash Register:

THE COUNTING MACHINE

How does a cash register keep track of all our purchases so that it comes up with the right amount we have to pay at the end?

Well, it all began in 1879 when an Ohio restaurant owner named Jake Ritty was on a ship heading for Europe. He loved machines and was able to persuade the captain to let him tour the engine room.

He was fascinated by one special machine that was constantly showing changing numbers on its dial.

"That," said the captain, "keeps track of the times the ship's propeller turns."

"A counting machine," Ritty thought. *"What if* I had a counting machine at the restaurant? I could add up the money my customers owed me accurately and quickly."

That night he worked out the idea in his head, and the next morning he began to put down plans on paper. When the ship landed in England, he got right back on another ship and headed home to start making a model of his own counting machine. He added a roll of paper to the machine and each time an amount was rung up, it was recorded on the paper. Because his machine kept a record of how much cash he took in each day, he called it a cash register.

Snowshoes:
THE RABBIT THAT FLEW OVER THE SNOW

The legends of the Native Americans who lived in what is today both the United States and Canada tell us a great deal about their history. They also tell us how these people observed nature and learned to use her secrets in their own lives.

One Native American legend that comes out of Canada deals with the experience of a man who went out into the middle of a lake one winter day and cut a hole in the ice to catch fish.

A sudden snowstorm came up as he

headed home with his catch. The snow piled up in deep drifts, and he sank down into them with every step he took.

He was growing tired and thought he might never get back to his warm lodge before the sun went down.

As he trudged along, he saw a fox peering out from behind a tree. The fox was staring at a rabbit just a few feet away. The fox was already on the move when the rabbit first noticed it. The man was sure the rabbit would soon become the fox's dinner.

But things didn't go quite that way. The fox kept sinking into the snow, while the rabbit skimmed over the snow, hardly making a mark in it as it moved along.

The man soon realized why the rabbit had the advantage. Unlike the fox with its small feet and thin legs, the rabbit's feet were long and wide. The weight of the rabbit was spread out over a larger area, making it harder for the rabbit to sink into the snow.

The man thought, "*What if* I made a pair of 'rabbit feet' for myself? Then I might be able to skim over the snow, too."

He took some twigs off a nearby tree and bent them into long oval shapes. He cut strips of leather from the sack in which he carried his fish and wove the strips back and forth to fill in the open spaces in each oval.

He tied his imitation rabbit feet onto his moccasins with two more strips of leather and then he tried them out.

Sure enough, instead of sinking in the snow, he was now able to walk on top of the deep drifts on what was the first pair of snowshoes.

Mailboxes:
GOING UP THE WALL

In the 1650s in Paris, the French government set up four post offices. This was a remarkable thing. For the first time the people of Paris had places to go to have their mail sent out all over France and Europe.

But there was no way for the people of Paris to send letters so easily between and among themselves. What they had to do was hire messengers to deliver their letters.

One day, in 1653, a man named Jean-Jacques Renouard de Villayer gave a messenger some letters to deliver. Then, the story goes, he took a walk around his neighborhood and noticed that on some corners, some nuns sat by baskets they set up to collect clothes to distribute to the poor. He thought, *"What if the city could set up baskets to collect letters that could then be distributed around Paris?"*

Soon, there were "wall boxes" set up on the corners of the main streets of Paris. People would wrap their letters in special ribbons marked Postage Paid, which they bought to use much as we use stamps today, and drop them into the boxes where they would be picked up three times a day and delivered. These wall boxes were the first mailboxes.

The Sewing Machine:

THE DREAM THAT TURNED INTO A SEWING MACHINE

Back in the 1830s, many people were working to invent a sewing machine. Elias Howe was one of those people. He was driven by a special reason: to help ease the burden on his wife, who worked long and hard into the night to sew clothes for the family.

He tried many different methods. But none of them worked very well. Then one day, while doing his regular work making watches and instruments for watchmaking, he had an idea: Watches work because of several movements that go on at the same time. He thought, "*What if* I made a machine with a needle that moved up and down and another needle that moved across at the same time?" But no matter how hard he tried, he just couldn't make his idea work the way he wanted it to.

Still, he wouldn't give up. He was like his name: When he faced a puzzling situation, he always said, "How can I do it?" and then he would find a way to answer his question. One night he dreamed of an arrow with a hole near the tip. When he awoke, he realized what he had seen in his dream. The arrow represented the needle, and the hole near the arrow tip showed him that what he had to do was put the eye of the needle near the point — not at the top where the eyes of regular needles are placed.

The new needle worked perfectly in the machine Howe had imagined. Elias Howe's sewing machine was a success; it really was a dream come true, in many ways.

French Fries:
BELGIAN FRIED
POTATOES

You probably have never really had French fried potatoes, although you think you have. You see, you may think the potatoes called French fries originally came from France. Well, they didn't. Which means they're not really French fries.

They were "invented" in Belgium by a cook who was cutting up several potatoes for use in a stew. As he moved the cut slices from the cutting board to the pot, most of them fell into a frying pan. He would have to throw these spoiled potatoes out. But he realized he had no more potatoes. His stew was ruined. What could he serve his guests instead?

The smell of the frying potatoes filled the kitchen. It was, the chef had to admit, a delicious smell.

He thought, "*What if* these frying potatoes taste as good as they smell?" He took one potato out, nibbled it, and smiled. "Oh yes," he said, "they are truly wonderful."

Everyone at the table agreed. They loved this new dish. Someone asked him what he called it. "*Pommes frites*," he said in French, which means fried potatoes.

Soon people were ordering fried potatoes in the French style. And that became French fried potatoes.

Levis and Jeans:
THE BLUES FOR GOLD

Levis or jeans: Whatever you call them, they're the most popular pants in the world.

It all started back in 1848 when people from all over the world rushed to California to mine for gold. A young New York cloth salesman named Levi Strauss decided to sell his wares out west as well. He packed a wagon of cotton, silk, wool, and canvas and headed for California. When he got there, he quickly sold out all the cloth he had, except for the canvas. Soon he had a store and was in business.

Many of his customers were miners who came in often because they always needed new pants to replace those that wore out so quickly in the mines.

Strauss thought, "*What if* I used the unsold canvas I've got on hand to make pants for the miners? This material is so strong, it's almost untearable."

He spotted some brass-headed nails he had bought for building a nice store counter someday. The nails gave him an idea: "*What if* I 'nail' the pockets on these pants so that they wouldn't tear with the weight of the tools the miners carry in them?"

Strauss took brass rivets, which were like nails, but shorter, and attached them along the pocket seams. The miners loved these new pants. Soon everyone wanted "Levi's trousers" or just plain "Levis."

He also used strong blue Italian cotton cloth to make pants for other people. This cloth came from Genoa in Italy and was called Genoese, pronounced jen-oh-eeze. People started saying the name quickly, and it became jeans.

The Two and a Half Million Year Old Bone:

THE TIME TRAVELER WITH THE COLD NOSE

Dr. Mary Leakey and her husband, Dr. Louis Leakey, were anthropologists. While some anthropologists study the way people live today, the Leakeys were anthropologists who devoted their lives to finding evidence about the ancestors of human beings and where and how they lived in prehistoric times.

In 1958 they came to a dry lake bed in Africa in a place called Olduvai Gorge to look for fossilized bones to prove their theory that human ancestry went back over a million years or more.

Since all dry lake beds were once muddy, they were good places to look for fossils because mud preserves bones very well.

The Leakeys spent months digging everywhere in the area, but found nothing. They were ready to pack up and leave — and would have left Olduvai Gorge forever — if Dr. Mary Leakey hadn't taken her dog, some say his name was Rex, for a late evening walk.

Within a half hour after Dr. Leakey clipped his leash on, Rex's cold nose would take Dr. Leakey back in time over a million years.

As they walked over the sandy lake bed, Rex sniffed the ground. Suddenly, he became quite excited. He started scratching at the earth. Dr. Leakey looked down. She could hardly believe her eyes. Rex seemed to be digging up a bone. But she and her husband had been in this very spot just three or four days earlier and found nothing!

Then she recalled there had been a furious cloudburst the day before. The whole area had been drenched. A nearby hill turned into a big sliding mud pile. She thought, *"What if* the rain had washed away some of the sand on this lake bed, exposing things that were buried before?"

Whatever it was that Rex sniffed out was now beginning to show itself as the dog's furious digging continued. Dr. Leakey got down and cleared away the last grains of sand covering the object.

There it was: a fossil bone and, obviously, a very old fossil bone at that.

Later, tests would confirm that Dr. Leakey's dog had helped her find an arm bone of a child who lived more than two and a half million years ago!

Skyscrapers:
THE MATCHSTICK HOUSE

Over one hundred years ago, no one could build a building over nine stories high. If they put just one brick to start the tenth floor, the walls might buckle under their own weight and come tumbling down.

In the late 1800s an architect named William LeBaron Jenney puzzled over the problem for months. One day he relaxed by building small structures out of matchsticks. When he had enough matchsticks stacked in a framework, he covered it with playing cards.

He had built a house! He thought, *"What if* I did the same with a real building? The matchsticks would be replaced by steel beams, and I'd cover the steel beam framework with bricks. In this way, I could build very tall buildings, indeed."

Jenney's design proved that a building could support a lot of weight if you built a framework first and then added the bricks or stone. (Next time you see a tall building going up, look at the beams they're putting up before they add the bricks or stone. This is the framework of the building. See how some beams go across, and some go up and down, and some connect with each other. This framework holds the weight of the building.) Jenney used his design to build the world's first skyscraper in Chicago in 1885. It was ten stories high. Today some skyscrapers tower over one hundred stories high, but they're still built on Jenney's principle of matchsticks and cards.

The Heimlich Maneuver:

DR. HEIMLICH'S MAGIC "PUSH"

Have you ever blown up a paper bag and then punched it? The loud noise is the sound of air rushing out. Well, Dr. Harry Heimlich tried to find a way to "punch" out the air in the lungs of a choking person. He knew that many people who choked to death on food or other objects stuck in their windpipes could have been saved if they had been able to clear their windpipes. He also knew that sometimes people who tried to help a choking person by slapping him or her on the back only made things worse.

After spending years as a chest surgeon, Dr. Heimlich had become a leading expert on how the lungs work. He knew that even a choking person usually had some air in his or her lungs. He thought, "*What if* I could find a way to get that air to come out of the lungs with such force, that it would push out whatever was stuck in the windpipe?"

He tried many methods and found one that came closest to what we do when we punch the air out of a paper bag.

Today, his method, the *Heimlich Maneuver* has saved many lives. Look for diagrams of the Heimlich Maneuver in restaurants. Also, ask your teacher or doctor to show you how to do the Maneuver properly. Someday it may help you save someone's life, maybe your own.

The Phonograph:
THE WORLD'S FIRST DISC JOCKEY

Thomas Alva Edison was the world's first disc jockey because *he was the first person to play a record!* He did more than that — he invented the phonograph. (Phonograph comes from two Greek words: *phono,* which means speech, and *graph,* which means to write.) A phonograph writes down speech, or records it, and also plays it back. It also records and plays back music and other sounds. While sending dots and dashes over a telegraph, Edison had wondered if the dots and dashes could be permanently recorded — and then played back. Edison knew the telegraph sent signals over a wire through an electrical current. But, he wondered, could signals also be carried by metal?

"What if," he said, "I attached a metal stylus, like a long, thin pen point, to my telegraph? And, *what if* I put a thin metal disk right under the point and have the disk rotate under it? Would it pick up the sound waves made by the dots and dashes and scratch them into the disk?" It did. Sounds were scratched into the disk by the stylus point. Then he had to find a way to "free" the sounds the stylus had "captured" so he could hear them. He put a needle at the end of an arm — something like the arm on your phonograph — which he suspended over the disk, and as it rotated, the needle moved along the grooves. But, the "free" sounds rushed into the arm, not his *ear*! He heard nothing. He wondered, "How do I get the *arm* to *talk* to me?" He recalled Alexander Graham Bell's telephone which carried

sound by means of a vibrating diaphragm made of a thin piece of iron. He thought, *"What if* I put a diaphragm at the point where the sound entered the arm? Would it act like a telephone and talk to me then?"* It did!

One day in 1877 he startled some friends when his voice came out of a box, saying, "Good morning — how do you like the phonograph?"

Edison soon thought of ten possible uses for his new invention:

1. Letter writing and all kinds of dictation without the aid of a stenographer.

2. Phonograph books that would speak to blind people.

3. The teaching of elocution.

4. Reproduction of music.

5. A family record to be a registry of remarks and reminiscences by family members, in their own voices and words.

6. Music boxes and toys.

7. Clocks that would announce the time.

8. The preservation of language by exact reproduction of pronounciation.

9. Educational purposes.

10. Connection with the telephone to make a permanent record of conversations.

Do any of these sound familiar to you?

Digitalis:

THE WITCH, THE DOCTOR, AND THE MAGIC CUP OF TEA

During the 1770s Dr. William Withering was one of the best doctors in England. As a scientist, he didn't believe in ghosts. Yet one day while he strolled through the village fair, he thought he saw a ghost . . . and then another one . . . and still another one. Five "ghosts" in all!

He stared in amazement. All of these people had been very ill with a disease called dropsy which caused liquid to form around a person's heart, leading to a heart attack. He had worried about them. But as good a doctor as he was, he had no way to treat them, and when they left his office, he was sure he'd never see any of them alive again.

But there they were, and they all looked very healthy. They told him about a wonderful "witch woman" who lived in a nearby wood. This "good witch," they said, had prepared a special brew which, they insisted, had cured them.

Dr. Withering was a very good scientist who knew the importance of investigating anything that sounded like a cure. He also knew that many remedies and medicines used by midwives and women healers (who were often called witches) could help cure illness and heal injuries. So, he decided to visit the "witch" and see what brews she was concocting.

Sure enough, when he got to her cottage she was busy making up her dropsy remedy out of some twenty plants, roots, berries, and herbs.

Dr. Withering asked for samples of many of her plants to study and after several tests, he decided that the most powerful plant in her brew had to be the herb foxglove. He thought, *"What if* there was something in the foxglove that cured the dropsy? And if so, what is it?"

Thanks to the "good witch," who was a healer, Dr. Withering was able to use his knowledge of botany to isolate the ingredient in the foxglove plant called digitalis, which may well be one of the most important natural products ever discovered for medicinal use. Today, digitalis in different forms is still a lifesaver used by doctors all over the world to help people with heart problems.

The Mackintosh Raincoat:

RAIN, RAIN GO AWAY . . .

Until a Scotsman named Mackintosh invented the raincoat named after him in the early 1800s, there was no way to stay really dry in the rain. That's because although a cotton coat dipped in latex, which is liquid rubber, could keep you dry, you wouldn't want to wear it. The latex would stiffen up quickly, and before long, you'd feel like a turtle in a shell made of hard rubber.

Mackintosh tried everything he knew to make latex rubber flexible enough to use as a coating for coats to be worn in Scotland where there are lots of heavy dews and fogs and rain. One story says he accidentally dropped a little latex on a cabinet top he had just brushed with turpentine to soften old varnish. He saw that the latex rubber, instead of hardening, stayed flexible. He thought, *"What if* the turpentine did this to the latex?"

He was right. He worked until he found the right turpentine and rubber combination. Then when he dipped cotton coats into the mixture, they stayed flexible as well as waterproof. Today, we still use the name mackintosh to describe a rubberized cotton raincoat.

The Assembly Line:

HENRY FORD AND THE "BELT THAT BUILT CARS"

In the early 1900s, automobiles cost a lot of money: Some of the best might be priced at five hundred dollars, an amount equal to what many people made in a year in those days. Those cars were built by hand and took weeks to complete.

A young man named Henry Ford started a car company in Detroit, Michigan. He began to look for a way to build lower-priced, good quality cars.

But how could he do this? He loved

machinery. Was there something he could build that would help him meet his goals?

He thought about the challenge. He remembered that when he was a young machinist's apprentice he learned how to build conveyor belt contraptions that were useful to carry heavy loads on farms. A conveyor belt is stretched over and around rollers at both ends. As the rollers turn, the belt moves.

A light bulb went off in Ford's head! That was it! He thought, "*What if* I built a conveyor belt the length of the factory? My workers would stand alongside the belt and work on parts of the cars as they passed along. It would be like putting a giant jigsaw puzzle together. At the end of the line, every piece of the car would be in place and the car would be fully assembled."

His assembly line worked, and it changed forever the way factories make their products.

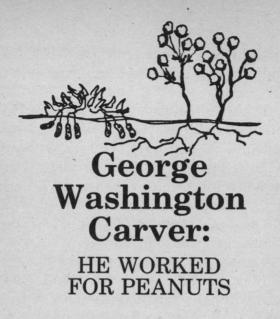

George Washington Carver:

HE WORKED FOR PEANUTS

Cotton is a greedy plant. It takes nutrients from the soil, particularly nitrogen, and gives nothing back. But for many years, farmers in the South grew mostly cotton, until the day came when almost nothing would grow, because all the nutrients were depleted.

But cotton was a "cash crop," a crop they could sell in the market to get money to buy the things they needed. Without cotton, the farmers had no cash to buy anything, not even food. And very little food could be grown in the tired earth.

George Washington Carver, a famous scientist who lived from 1864 to 1943, was a southerner, the son of former slaves. As a southerner, he knew the importance of the cash crop. From his research, he also knew that legumes — such as cowpeas, beans, and peanuts — take nitrogen from the air and release it into the soil through their roots. But how could he get the farmers to plant peanuts to help put nitrogen and other nutrients back into the worn-out soil? He thought, *What if* I can find a way to make peanuts a cash crop, too?"

He experimented with peanuts and made over three hundred products including shampoo, shaving cream, paint, cooking oil, soap, and even a kind of rubber made from the peanut hulls. Because of his experiments, farmers all over the South began to plant peanuts. Peanuts became the sixth largest crop grown in the United States. The peanuts improved the soil, and in time, cotton could be grown in it again.

"From now on," Dr. Carver said, "we can plant peanuts not just for what they give *us*, but also for what they give to the earth."

The Bubonic Plague:

HOW TO MAKE THE FLEAS FLEE

About five hundred years ago a disease called the black death — also known as bubonic plague — swept Europe. No place seemed safe from it. But, one story goes, the Jews who lived in a ghetto in Strasbourg didn't catch the disease.

The people outside the ghetto were angry. "How come," they asked, "we get the plague and the Jews don't?" Someone asked, "Are the Jews practicing witchcraft?"

The town priest, Father Pierre, who was a great scholar and often studied the Old Testament said, "I'll visit them and see what the truth is."

The Jewish leaders welcomed Father Pierre and introduced him to their doctor, Dr. Bevignus, who invited him to look around the ghetto.

Father Pierre made notes of the fact that every day, everyone took their garbage out to a place at the edge of the ghetto and dumped it into a fire that was constantly burning. The surprised priest asked, "Why do you do this?"

"It is our religious law," Dr. Bevignus said, "and it is also a health law."

Father Pierre was even more shocked to notice there were no rats to be seen. Yet, there were so many rats everywhere else!

"Why is this so?" he asked.

"Because," Dr. Bevignus said, "rats eat garbage, and we have no garbage for them to eat. As you see, we burn our garbage every day."

Father Pierre thought, "*What if* burning the garbage really is the key to keeping the plague away?"

He rushed back to his part of Stras-bourg and told the people there to burn their garbage every day as well. Sure enough, within weeks, fewer and fewer people got the disease. Soon, no one got it at all.

Today we know why burning garbage worked so well. Rats carried the flea that carried the germ that caused the disease. No garbage. No rats. No fleas. No plague.

The Shopping Cart:

TURNING ON CARTWHEELS

During the late 1930s, Sylvan N. Goldman, a supermarket manager of a Humpty Dumpty store in Oklahoma City wondered what he could do to help his customers with their purchases. Even those who had shopping baskets sometimes were unable to get them to the cash register because they were filled and heavy.

As he walked to work one day, he saw two folding chairs facing each other on a lawn. "That's it," he thought.

"*What if* I put two folding chairs together, put wheels on them, and put a strip of wood on the seat and put more strips of wood around the sides like a crib? Then it would become a giant basket my customers could move around like a baby carriage!"

On June 4, 1937, he introduced a "cartwheel," the world's first supermarket shopping cart on wheels.

The Lightning Rod:

BENJAMIN FRANKLIN'S SHOCKING DISCOVERY

Benjamin Franklin didn't discover electricity. Scientists in America and Europe were studying this strange force for many years. Even the ancient Greeks knew about it three thousand years ago when they entertained children by rubbing amber jewelry until it attracted pieces of cloth. But Benjamin Franklin was the first person to say that lightning was electricity — and he could prove it.

He started his experiments with electricity in the 1740s. By 1748 he found the way to prove lightning was really an electrical charge. He took an iron key and tied it to the end of a kite string. He did this because he knew electric currents flow toward metal. He then let the kite fly into a lightning storm. Sure enough, the lightning was attracted to the key. It traveled down the string and when it hit the key, he felt an electric shock as a spark flared up, proving that lightning is electricity.

Franklin was very lucky that night: The electric charge could have killed him. But he didn't know that then. What he did realize was that he had found a way to "collect" electricity. This meant there was a chance to catch it — and get rid of it — before it could kill people or destroy houses or barns.

He thought, "The big problem with lightning is that no one knows where it will strike, so no one can be prepared for it. But, *what if* I could catch lightning with a much longer 'key' *before* it struck a person or an animal or a house?"

He tied a long metal rod to the chimney on his roof. He was told it was useless: No one could ever control where or when lightning would strike. But when it stormed again, his lightning rod attracted the bolt, making the lightning harmless by keeping it from striking anything else around it. Today, lightning rods protect buildings from lightning. Do you know of any buildings with lightning rods on them?

X rays:

X MARKS THE SPOT

Less than one hundred years ago, no one knew about the X ray until a German scientist who was experimenting with light discovered it accidentally.

Konrad Roentgen was in his laboratory one day in 1895 working to find why certain substances react to different lightwaves. He put a piece of paper covered with a fluorescent substance into a cathode ray tube. The paper glowed. But why? What made it glow?

He realized that a mysterious ray that he had never encountered before was causing the glow. Since he knew nothing about it, he called it the X ray because in mathematics, the letter X always stands for the unknown.

Because most of Roentgen's work with light involved photography, he thought, *"What if* I used this mystery ray in a special camera? Would it produce a photograph the way other light waves do? Or would it produce something else? Or maybe it would produce nothing at all?"

Roentgen often discussed his work with his wife and although Christmas was only three days away and she was very busy, she took time to listen to his idea.

Frau Roentgen was intrigued by his idea: She agreed with him that photography was a good way to try to find how this strange light force worked, and she suggested that he take a picture of her hand, and when it was developed, they could write down the date — December 22, 1895 — on which this mysterious light source was used for the first time to take photographs.

Roentgen focused his camera on his wife's hand and took the picture. When he developed it he found, to his amazement, that this unknown light ray had penetrated the flesh on Frau Roentgen's hand, producing a picture of her finger bones and of the wedding ring on one of her fingers.

Today, X rays are used in medicine, science, agriculture, and technology.

Cheese:
HOW CHEESE WAS INVENTED

Cheese making began over one thousand years ago with the Mongolian nomads who wandered the great plains of Asia. They loved milk which they got from their camels and mares. When a camel died, they would clean its stomach and fill it with water or milk to drink along the way. They then tied it to their saddles when they traveled across the land. Sometimes there were traces of enzymes still left in the cleaned stomach sacs.

Enzymes are substances which help

digest food by changing its form. And, sometimes, the sacs that still had traces of these digestive fluids in them caused the milk to change into a curdlike substance as it sloshed and splashed inside as the animals moved along.

At first, the nomads thought the milk was spoiled, and they would throw the curds away. But they noticed that their dogs would lick up the discarded curds and seemed to thrive on them.

Some of the nomads thought, *"What if* we tried to eat this curdled milk, too?"

Well, of course, when they tried it, they found it very tasty. Soon everyone who sampled it agreed it was too good a food to throw out anymore.

In time, people learned how to make cheese by using enzymes, *without* using animal stomachs. The milk of many different animals, including goats, sheep, and cows, is used to make hundreds of kinds of cheese.

Penicillin:

GOOD THING HE DIDN'T DO THE DIRTY DISHES THAT NIGHT!

It's a good thing English scientist Dr. Alexander Fleming didn't wash a very important dirty dish one night in his laboratory. If he had, he might never have found the miracle cure that has saved millions of lives since he made his discovery in the 1920s.

Dr. Fleming had spent years searching for a way to fight deadly infections. To do this he had to study the same bacteria that caused these infections. That meant he needed to have a large supply on hand at all times. To grow the bacteria, he put them into culture dishes which he filled with the food that helped them grow and multiply.

One night a tiny mold spore carried by the wind blew into his laboratory and somehow got into a culture dish. The next day, Dr. Fleming was shocked to find a huge splotch of mold growing all over the inside of the dish.

"This is terrible," he said to himself. "I'll have to wash this dish later and start over again." He set the dish down and came back in an hour. He looked. "What's this? Where are the bacteria? They're gone. Where did they go?"

He thought, "Ummm, *what if* the *mold* has eaten them? I'll put more mold into another bacteria batch and see what happens."

Sure enough, the mold gobbled the bacteria as happily as his cat lapped up her daily dish of cream. He used this mold, which is called *Penicillium,* to make a medication he named penicillin. After many tests, in 1928 he told the world it now had a powerful weapon to fight many once deadly infections. Dr. Fleming won a Nobel Prize for his discovery of this potent antibiotic.

Frozen Food:
HOW DRY WE ARE

In 1912 Clarence Birdseye left his home in Brooklyn and went to Labrador in northern Canada. He saw that whenever his Eskimo friends caught more fish than they needed, they hung the fish on a line stretched between two tall poles, instead of wrapping them up in ice to preserve them. In about fifteen minutes, the fish froze hard as a rock, and stayed frozen until they were taken down for the next meal.

Birdseye was impressed. He decided that when he got back to the United

States, he'd find a way to freeze all kinds of foods so that people could enjoy them at any time of the year.

When Birdseye returned home in 1916, he started working on quick-freeze systems. But sometimes his methods took 18 hours or more and the food often tasted pretty bad when it was thawed out.

One cold winter's day, it is said, he saw laundry hanging on a line. The clothes were frozen stiff. The line reminded him of the frozen fish in Labrador. "*What if,*" Birdseye said to himself, "the fish froze because they were hung up to 'dry' first? *What if* that's the secret to freezing food successfully?"

And, indeed, that was the secret. Finally, Clarence Birdseye found a way to get most of the moisture out of food before freezing. And in 1949, he introduced a whole menu of frozen food.

Magainin:
THE FROGS WITH THE HEALING SHIELDS

Dr. Michael Zasloff of the Institute for Child Health and Human Development found that frogs have shields.

It all began when Dr. Zasloff wondered why injured frogs got better quickly, and without any infections, although they never got any antibiotics. "Why is this happening?" he asked.

Up until Dr. Zasloff asked that question, scientists took for granted that a frog's wounds healed naturally and quickly without antibiotics. But Dr. Zasloff wanted to know why this was so.

He examined each frog carefully. He thought, "there must be something shielding them from infection, and it has to be a very big shield to fight against so many dangerous germs."

A big shield? Suddenly, Dr. Zasloff had the clue he was looking for. He knew the biggest shield any creature has against infection is a healthy skin. When it's unbroken it keeps most germs out. When it is broken, we clean it with an antiseptic or antibiotic to make sure it doesn't get infected while it heals. Dr. Zasloff thought, *"What if* the answer is in the skin of these lucky frogs?"

Sure enough, in 1987, he isolated two very important chemicals which he named *magainins* — the Hebrew word for shield. This breakthrough natural antibiotic was the frog's shield against infection.

How important are magainins? No one knows yet. You are one of the first to know about it.

But some of the greatest discoveries and inventions have come from pure science: Looking at things in a different way and asking, *"What if"* — and in the blink of an eye, changing the world.